A PERSONAL COLLECTION OF FINGER-STYLE GUITAR MUSIC

Parlors, Porches & Islands

BY DOC ROSSI

ISBN 978-1-57424-400-7
SAN 683-8022

Copyright © 2021 CENTERSTREAM Publishing
P.O. Box 17878 - Anaheim Hills, CA 92817

www.centerstream-usa.com | centerstrm@aol.com | 714-779-9390

I have broken the pieces down into sections to help you learn them faster.
For complete performances of the pieces in this book, look for
Parlors Porches & Islands at
docrossimusic.com

Audio Track List

Photos of Doc by João Paulo Lima

Contents

Introduction

I started playing the guitar in 1967, when musical eclecticism ruled. Not only was there great FM radio in Detroit back then, but my local library had a surprising collection of LPs that fired my curiosity further. The affinity I developed early on with Irish and English traditional music grew out of my first falling in love with the dance music of medieval, renaissance and baroque Europe. Although I came of age during a time of cultural revolution, I also developed a deep reverence for the past through the music that captivated me, which has in turn led me to the countries from which it flows.

Roots can be tough, tangled and gritty, and they don't always reveal what we might expect. Some people might be disappointed at finding the roots of blues and old-time guitar playing in bourgeois parlor music, but it fascinates me. Like Joseph Campbell says, it's what we share in common that is most revealing. Although my musical roots are firmly in America, my travels have led to an appreciation of many kinds of traditional and "art" musics. In this collection I've tried to blend the ancient sounds of early music, the intricacies of traditional dance music, and the mystery of "Old Weird America".

This collection is a voyage from 18th-century country dance tunes to 19th-century parlor or domestic guitar music, to music that found its way to traditional rural players, to Slack Key players in Hawai'i, and from there to my own music. Along the way we'll use some of the most important open tunings that have come down to us today.

Tablature

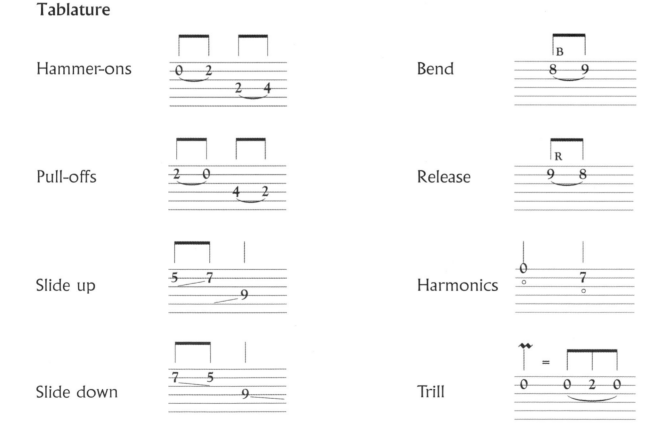

There are only a few places where I've put in right-hand fingerings. Where these occur, I use standard classical guitar letters to indicate the fingers:

p = thumb   *i* = index   *m* = middle   *a* = ring

Old Open G - G B D G B D

The first group of pieces are in a tuning I call Old Open G. It is more or less standard tuning today for Bluegrass and country steel guitar or Dobro players, but in fact this tuning actually comes from the 18c cittern, also known as the English guittar *[sic]*, an instrument that was popular from about 1750 to about 1850. These instruments came in various sizes, and were tuned accordingly. The most common was C, followed by A and G. The 7-string Russian guitar uses the same G tuning with the addition of a lower D bass.

In addition to dropping the top E down to D, the low E has to go up to G, and the A up to B. Obviously, the lower strings have to be light enough to get there. If your strings aren't light enough, you can drop the whole tuning down by one or two semitones or frets.

The so-called English guittar was a very popular domestic instrument in 18c Europe, used to play popular songs, light classical, and country dance tunes.

Preston guittar c.1760 tuned in C

Gibson guittar c.1770 tuned in G

The Princess Royal & Poll Ha'penny

I first learned this version of "The Princess Royal" from Michael Plunkett and Paul Gross of The Rakes, a traditional group from London who, together with Reg Hall and Lucy Farr, took me under their collective wing and gave me a real education in traditional music making. Michael and Paul learned the tune from a McCusker Brothers' broadcast on the BBC. It shares its title with a piece attributed to Irish harper Turlough O'Carolan, but is different from his.

Another 18c Irish tune, "Poll Ha'penny" is reputed to have been O'Carolan's favorite tune - he reportedly said he would rather have written it than all the other tunes he composed. It makes a good companion piece to "The Princess Royal."

The Drunken Sailor

Not the popular song, but a 19c Irish hornpipe also known as "The Groves." The alternate D part has a contemporary harmonization. I usually play this twice, finishing with a final A.

The Princess Royal

Trad. arr. Doc Rossi

Guitar Tuning
G B D G B D

Poll Ha'penny

Trad. arr. Doc Rossi

Guitar Tuning
G B D G B D

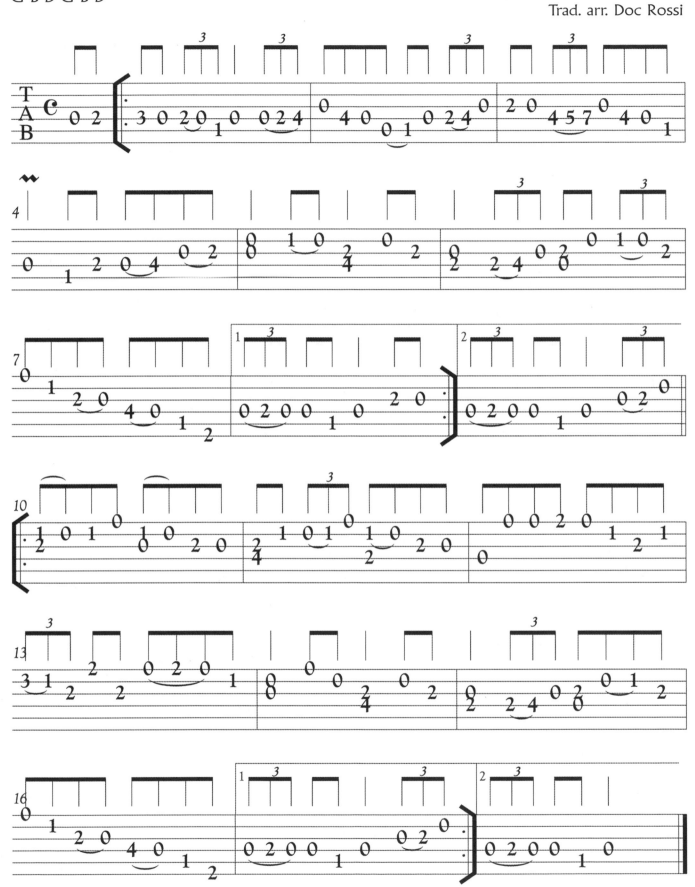

The Drunken Sailor

Guitar Tuning
G B D G B D

Trad. arr. Doc Rossi

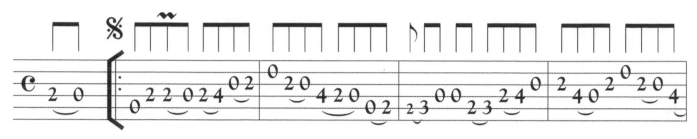

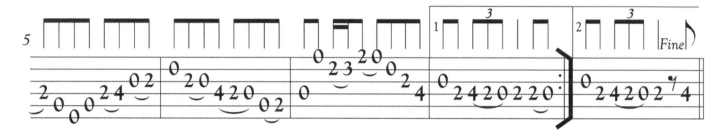

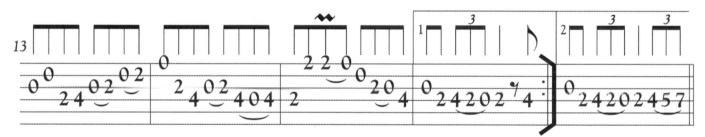

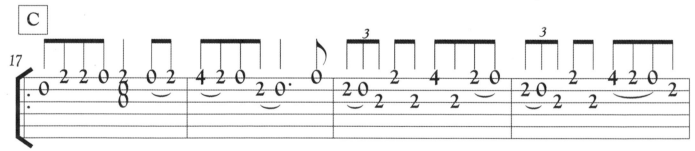

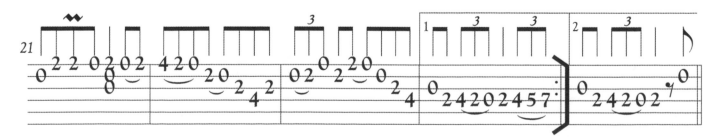

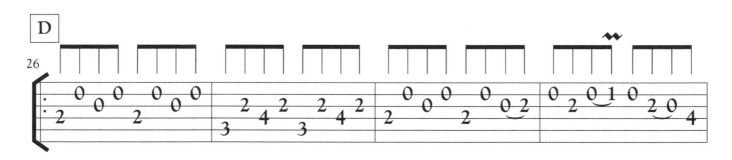

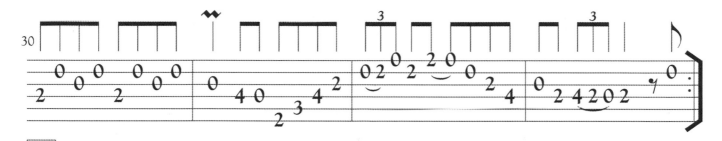

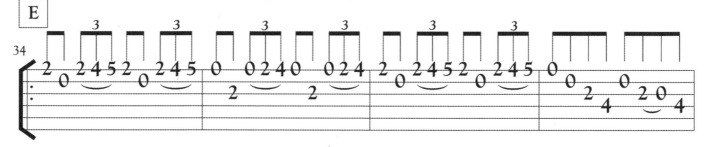

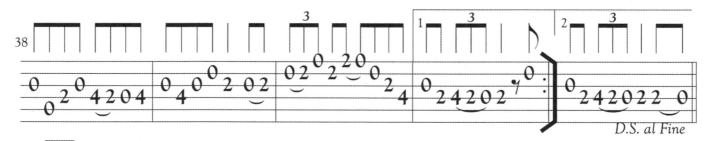

D.S. al Fine

Alt.

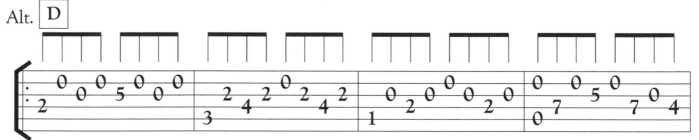

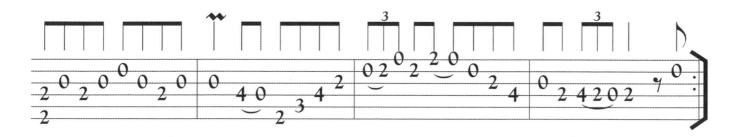

Spanish/Taro Patch/Open G - D G D G B D

The next tuning is Open G, also known as Spanish tuning because the famous Spanish Fandango is played in this tuning. It is one of the earliest and most common alternative tunings for the guitar, used by Norman Blake, John Renbourn, Ry Cooder, Keith Richards, to name but a few. Spanish tuning is known as Taro Patch among Slack Key or *ki ho'alu* guitarists because it is as common as the taro, the traditional staple food of Hawai'i.

Henry Worrall

Liverpool-born Henry Worrall immigrated to Cincinnati, Ohio in about 1835 - not far, by the way, from Dayton, where I was born. An accomplished artist and illustrator, he taught music at the Ohio Female College, and in 1856 published *Worrall's Guitar School, or The Eclectic Guitar Instructor.* Four years later he registered the copyright for two compositions, pieces of guitar music destined to have long and far-reaching influence on American vernacular guitar playing. One of these was "Worrall's Original Spanish Fandango" (first page below), in open G tuning; the other was "Sebastopol, Descriptive Fantaisie for the Guitar" in open D (see p. 24).

However, if you look through Worrall's *Guitar School,* "Sebastopol" is already there, as is a little piece called "Violet Waltz" (see below), which uses the same tuning and melodic material as "Spanish Fandango."

Worrall's Original Spanish Fandango

Although not very interesting on its own, it would be hard to over-emphasize how important this piece has been for American Blues and Old-Time Country guitar players, not to mention their descendants. This arrangement gives the first two sections, the same as in "Violet Waltz".

A word about *ki ho'alu* - Slack Key Guitar

Guitars came to Hawai'i sometime in the early 19th century, either with European sailors and other visitors, with Hawai'ians returning to the islands from the continent, or with Californian and Mexican cowboys - *vaqueros* - who were invited to teach Hawai'ians how to deal with their cattle. Open tunings are common in Mexico, and *vaqueros* could have passed them on to Hawai'ians, but what is clear is that Hawai'ians began fingerpicking and experimenting with open tunings almost immediately.

In the beginning, guitars on the islands were gut strung, but there is evidence that steel-string guitars began to arrive by the 1880s, probably with Portuguese immigrants, as Portugal has a long tradition of *violas arame* or metal-string guitars. One of these instruments was the *braguinha*, which morphed into the *'ukulele,* or jumping flea, in Hawai'i. The steel string guitar eventually became the dominant instrument in *ki ho' alu,* and helped in the creation and development of the steel guitar.

Slack key remained an Hawai'ian secret until the first commercial recordings were released in 1946-7, but it didn't really gain international acclaim until the 1970s during the Hawai'ian Cultural Renaissance.

Slack Key Study

This little piece is designed to show you some typical hammer-on and pull-off licks, slides and harmonics used by countless Slack Key players to imitate the falsetto singing, yodelling and other vocal effects of ancient Hawai'ian chants and songs. Entire pieces have been created based on these simple, effective ideas.

Slack Key Hula

Originally recorded in the late 1940s or early '50s, George Keoki Davis's "Slack Key Hula" is one of the first *ki ho' alu* pieces I learned. Included on Folklyric's *Hawaiian Steel Guitar 1920's-1950's* (1976), it hit me as soon as I heard it, and sent me on my journey to find more *ki ho'alu.* I haven't put all of the hammer-ons and pull-offs so as to keep the music uncluttered. Take your cue from "Slack Key Study," and use them wherever you like.

Hawai'ian Fandango

Based on Worral's "Spanish Fandango", this piece evokes some of the character of Slack Key guitar in terms of ornaments, phrasing, and general feel. It's a natural for *ki ho' alu,* and shows a clear link to parlor guitar music.

I like to start with the shortened version of "Spanish Fandango" then go into this piece.

Spanish Fandango

Guitar Tuning
D G D G B D

Henry Worrall
arr. Doc Rossi

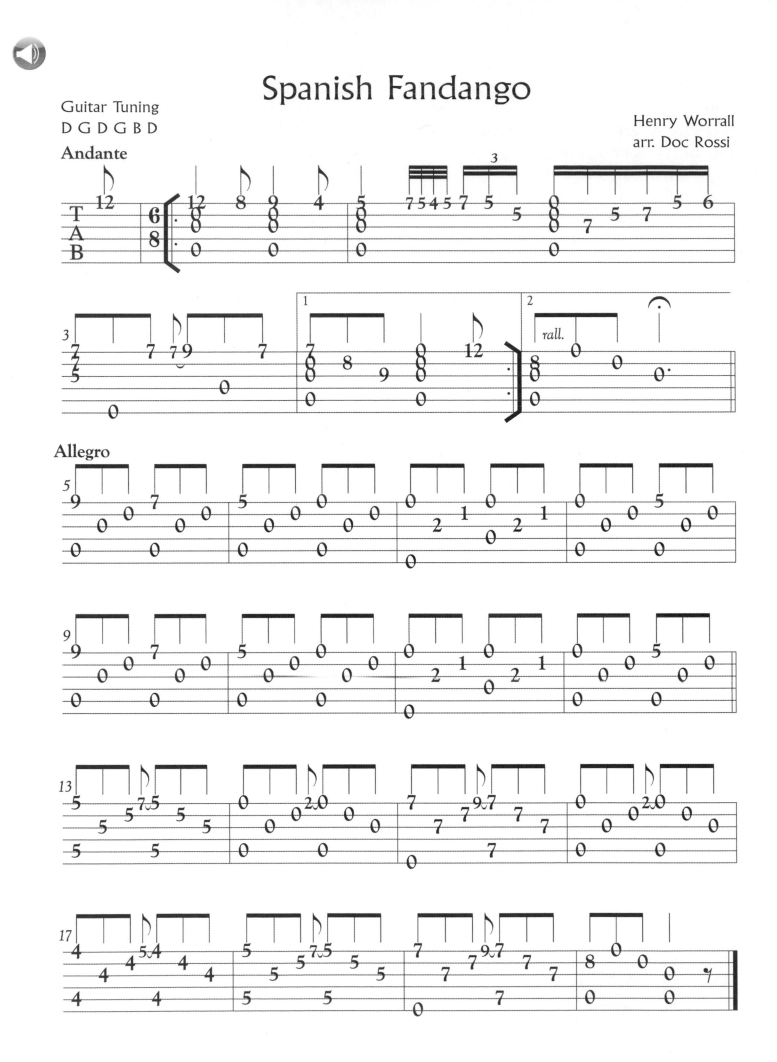

Slack Key Study

Guitar Tuning
D G D G B D

Trad. arr. Doc Rossi

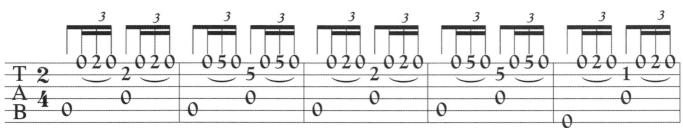

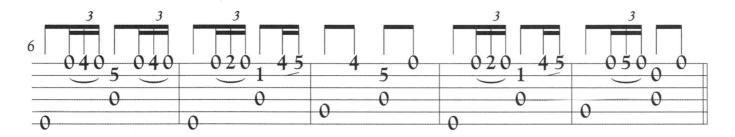

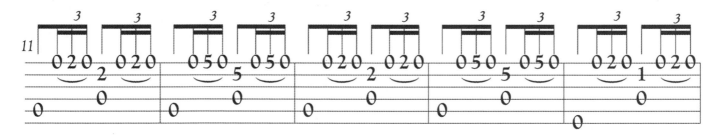

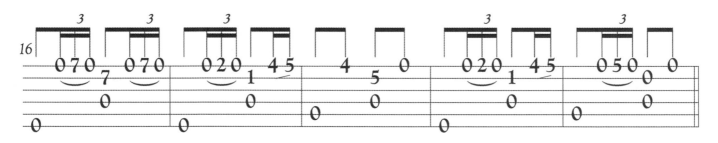

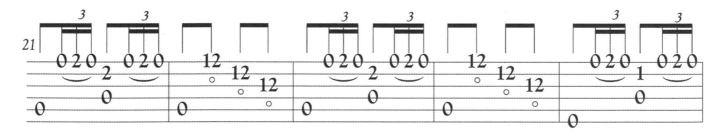

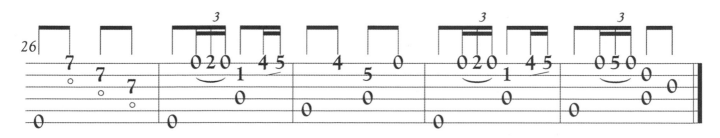

Slack Key Hula

Guitar Tuning
D G D G B D₃

Trad. arr. Doc Rossi

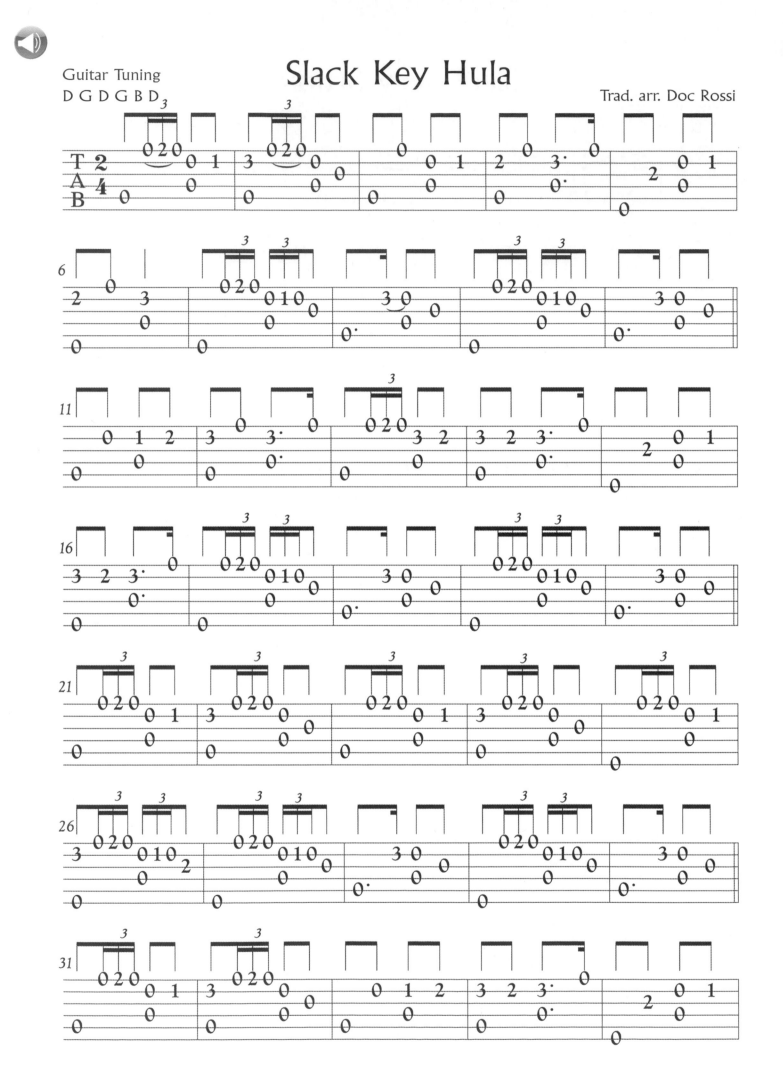

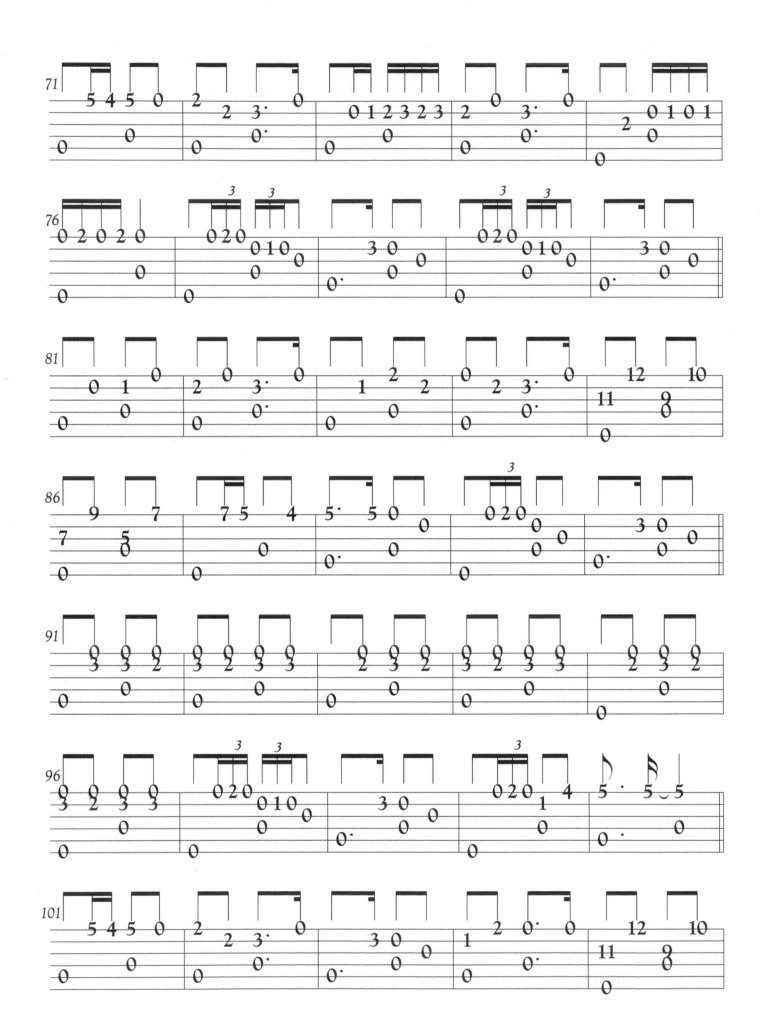

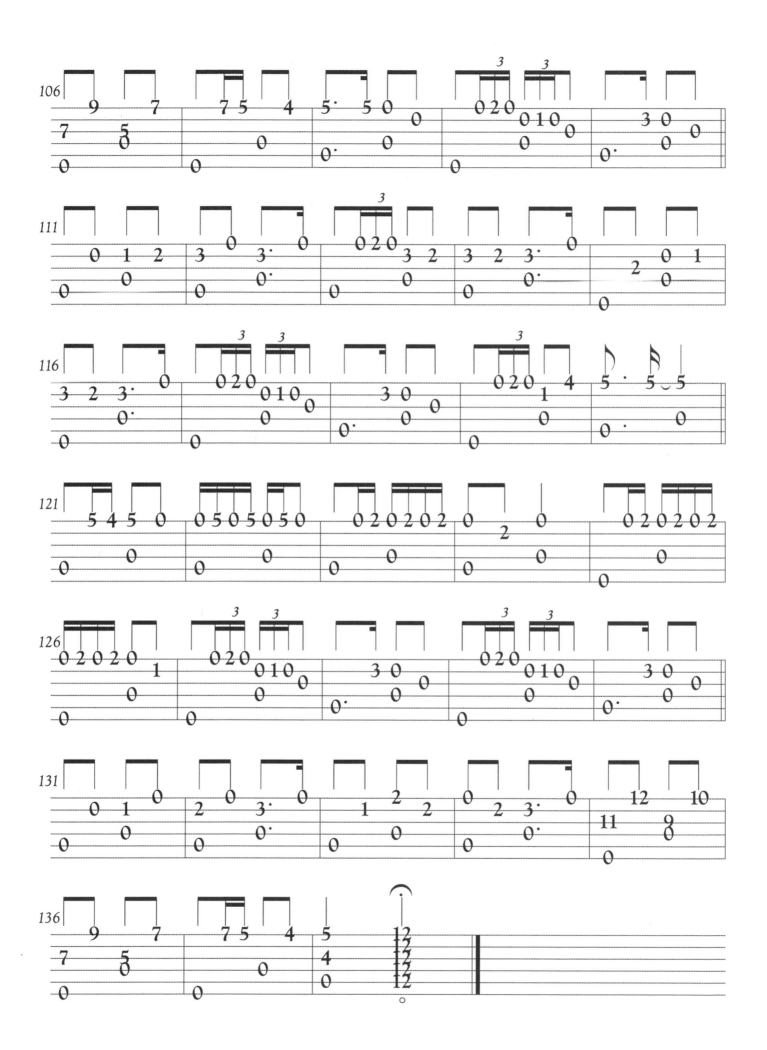

Hawai'ian Fandango

Guitar Tuning
D G D G B D

Doc Rossi

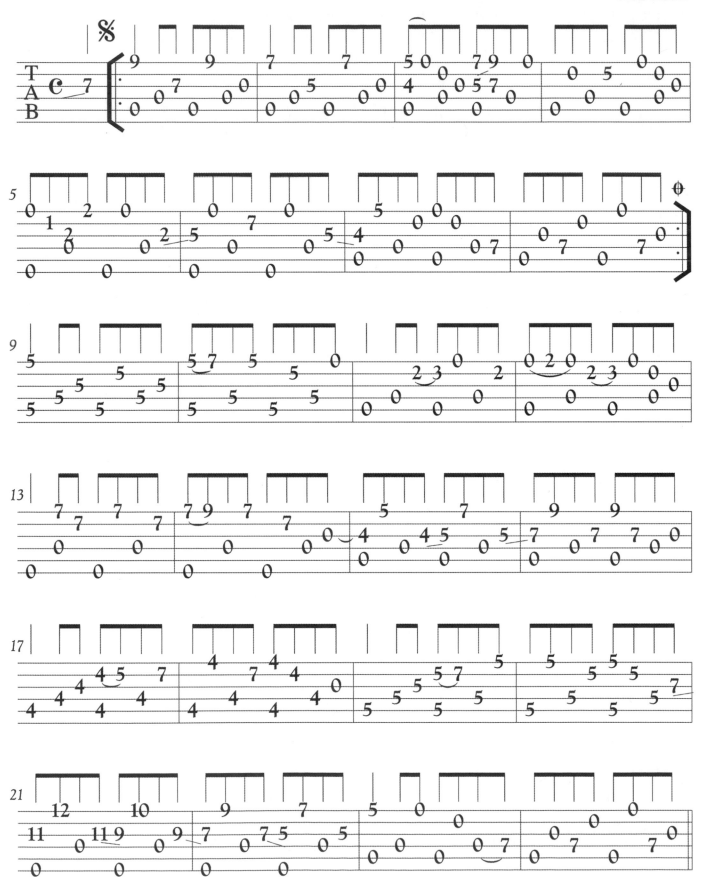

Variations

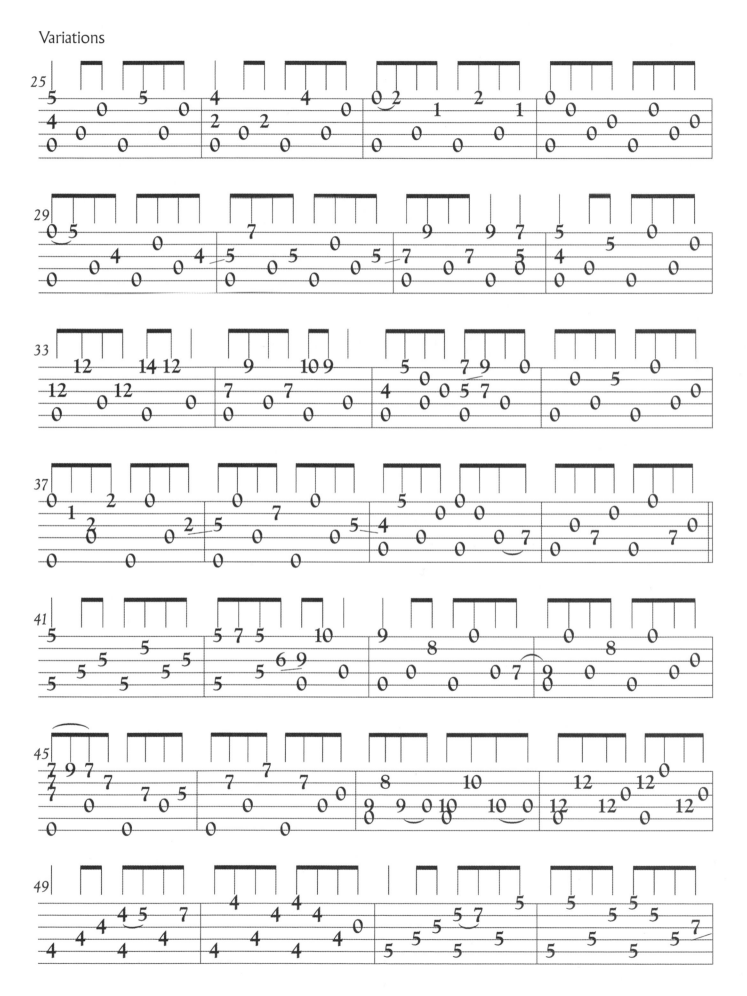

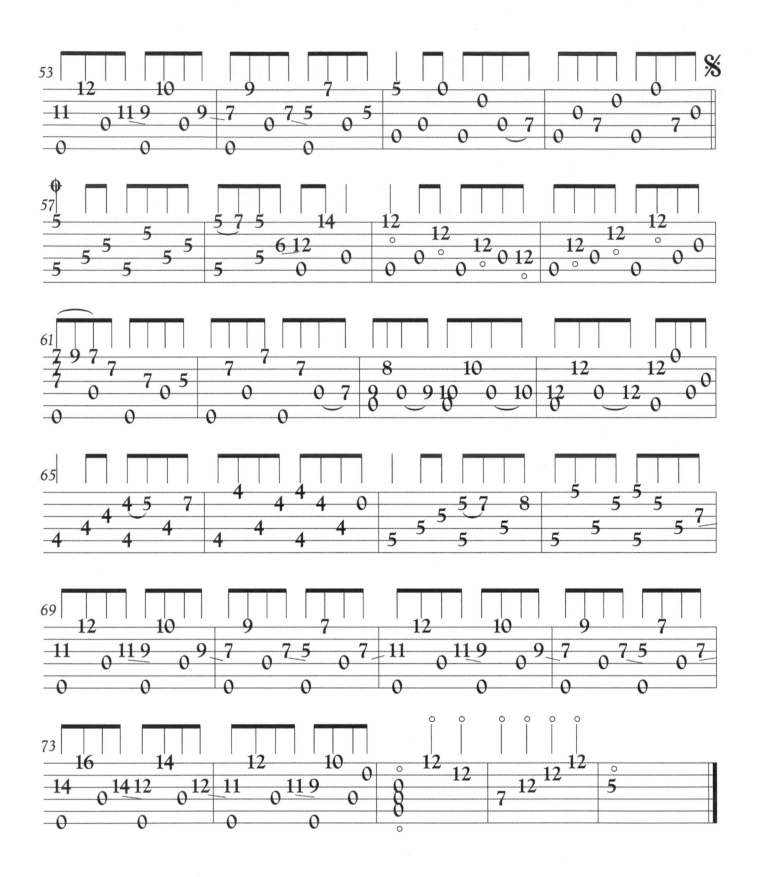

G Modal - D G D G C D

Once in open G, tune the second string up one semitone or fret to C and you are in G Modal tuning. Known as Sawmill among Old-Time 5-string banjo players, it's used for classics like Hobart Smith's "Cuckoo Bird," and was adapted to the guitar by players like Roscoe Holcomb, while John Renbourn used it for medieval music. With "Sarung Banggi" I use it to play a romantic, Spainish-influenced ballad from the *harana* tradition of serenading in the Philippines.

Sarung Banggi (One Evening)

This is one of the most loved songs in Philippine folk music, and has a strong Spanish influence. As the Philippines were under Spanish rule for more than three centuries, it should be no surprise that Spanish influence is everywhere, no less In the islands' traditional music. *Harana* comes from the Spanish word *jarana* and refers to a Spanish baroque guitar that has become a folk instrument in Mexico.

Although the song is now considered traditional, it was written by Potenciano Gregorio near the end of the 19th century. There are two stories about its creation; one is that he wrote it after listening to a bird singing one evening; the other is that he wrote it for his girlfriend after the Mount Mayon volcano had erupted.

The photo below shows a typical *harana* serenade in the Philippines. In addition to the usual guitars, one of the men appears to be playing a Mexican *guitarron*.

Sarung Banggi
One Evening

Guitar Tuning
D G D G C D

Trad. arr. Doc Rossi

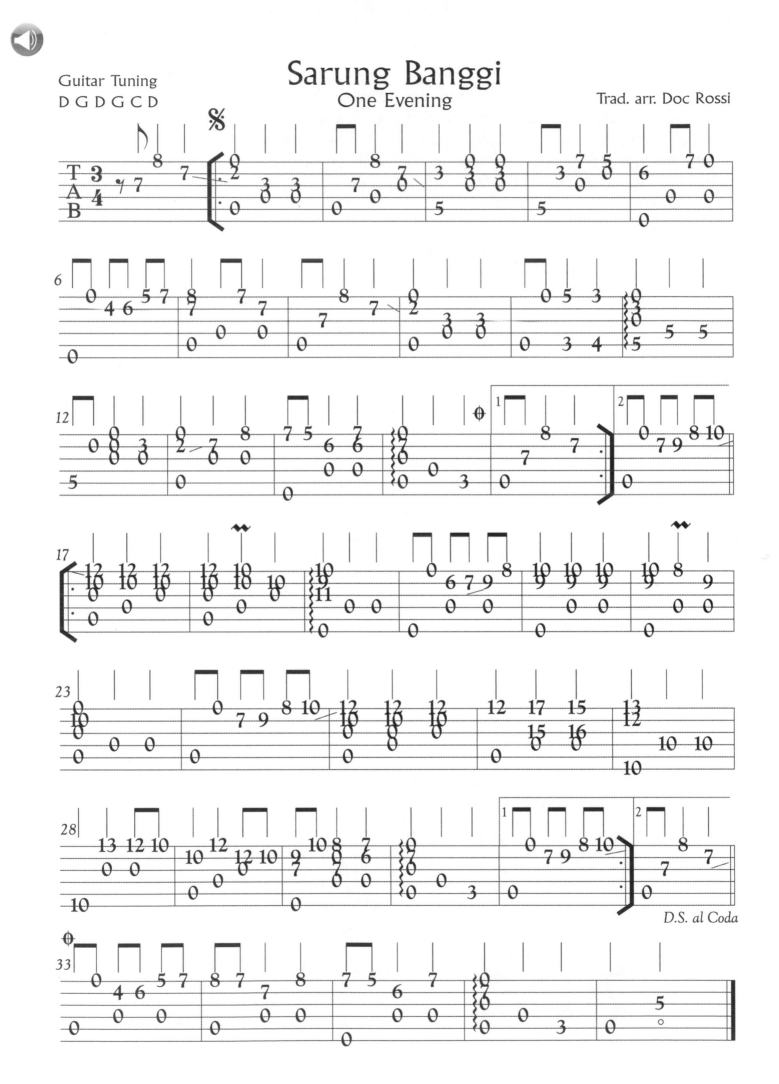

Vestapol/Open D - D A D F# A D

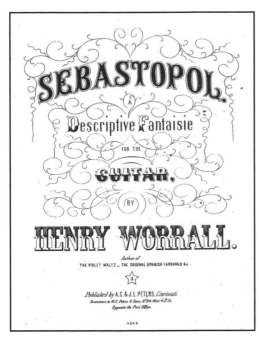

Along with open G, Vestapol, or open D, is one of the earliest and most common alternative tunings for guitar, and once again is associated with one of Henry Worrall's iconic guitar arrangements. A great tuning for finger-style arrangements, it's been a favorite with the like of John Fahey and Joni Mitchell, as well as slide players like Ry Cooder, Duane Allman and Elmore James.

Sebastopol, Descriptive Fantaisie for the Guitar

The other piece Henry Worrall registered on that fateful day in 1860 was "Sebastopol, Descriptive Fantaisie for the Guitar" in open D tuning. As I note above, "Sebastopol" appeared in his *Guitar School* four years earlier, in much the same form. I usually play just the first three parts, leaving out the imitations of bugles and distant bands.

Sailing out of Sebastopol I, II, III

My arrangement of "Sailing out of Sebastopol" starts with the original, then continues with a reprise of the first three parts of the original played with a funkier American Primitive feel (Part I). It then goes on to quote from pieces that sailed out of Worrall's original before circling back to it to Part I, and finally a reprise of the original played faster. We can hear elements of several fingerpicking classics like "Poor Boy" (Part II) and "Steel Guitar Rag" (Part III).

The first page of "Sebastopol" from Worrall's *Guitar School*.

Homage to Clarence White

I bought Arlo Guthrie's *Running Down the Road* when it came out in 1969. The intro to the first track, played by Clarence White, literally knocked me out of my chair. I'd never heard a feel like that before, and Clarence's music has been with me every day since. The way he tried to paint himself into a corner and always escape still amazes me. Celebrating his playing from the perspective of American Primitive fingerpicking, this piece uses material from John Dilleshaw's 1929 recording of "Spanish Fandango", played here in open D rather than open G. I play this piece straight through, then repeat section B and finish with section A.

From the Mysterious South [for Norman and Nancy Blake]

Like the music of Clarence White, the music of Norman and Nancy Blake has been with me every day since I sat at their feet for a duo gig at The Ark in Ann Arbor, Michigan in the 1970s. These two old-time tunes celebrate two great players and composers.

Kettle Drum

Despite its title, this is a lovely, lilting dance tune from the 50s - the 1650s, that is - played in American Primitive style, and sounding a bit like a Rock 'n' Roll ballad from the 1950s. It also demonstrates how easy it is to play in the key of A in open D tuning.

Sebastopol

Guitar Tuning
D A D F# A D

Henry Worrall
arr. Doc Rossi

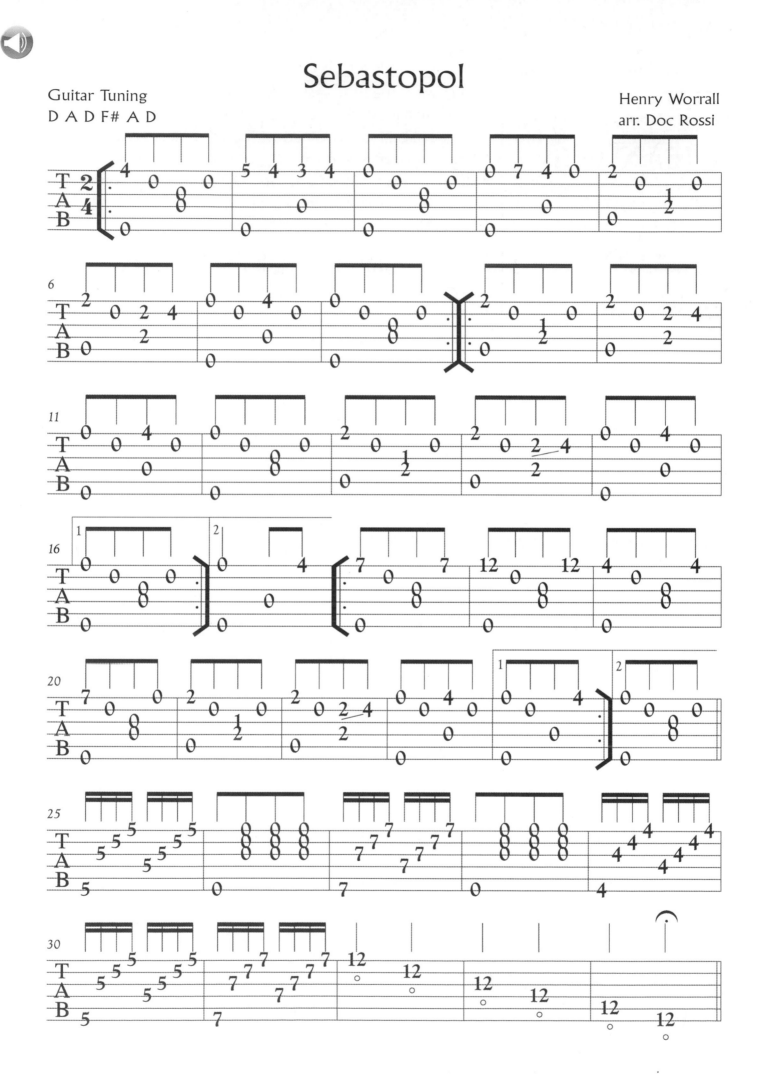

Sailing out of Sebastopol
Part I

Guitar Tuning
D A D F# A D

Trad. arr. Doc Rossi

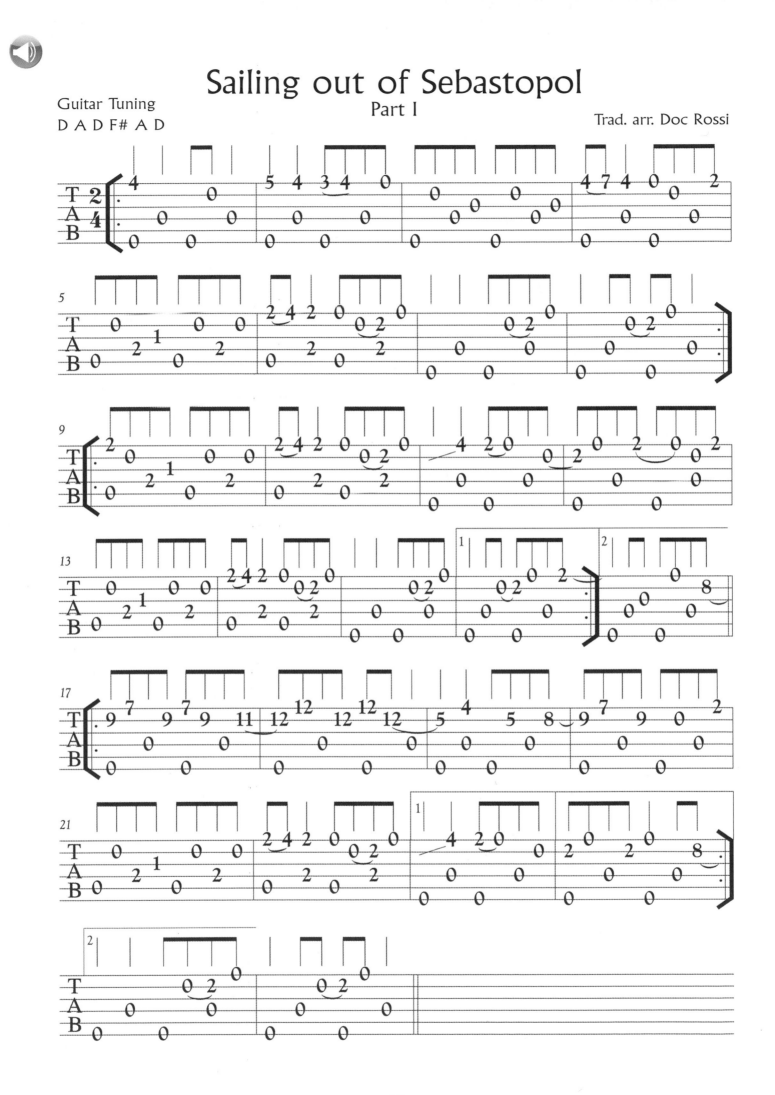

Sailing out of Sebastopol
Part II

Guitar Tuning
D A D F# A D

Trad. arr. Doc Rossi

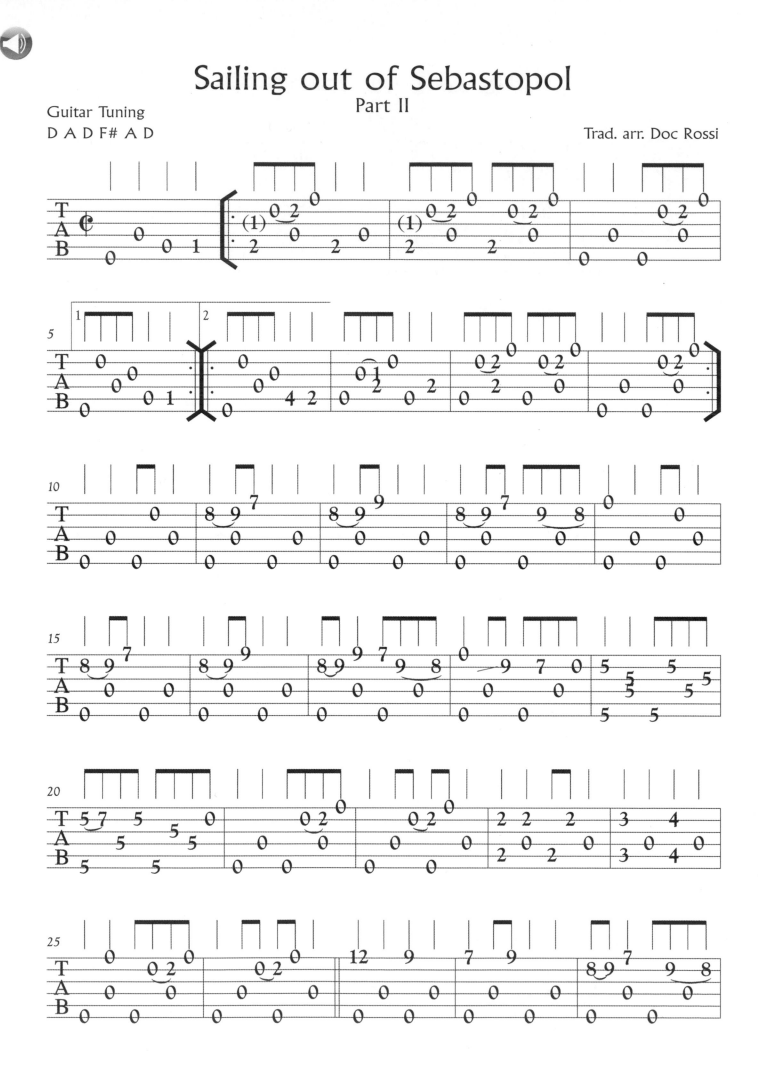

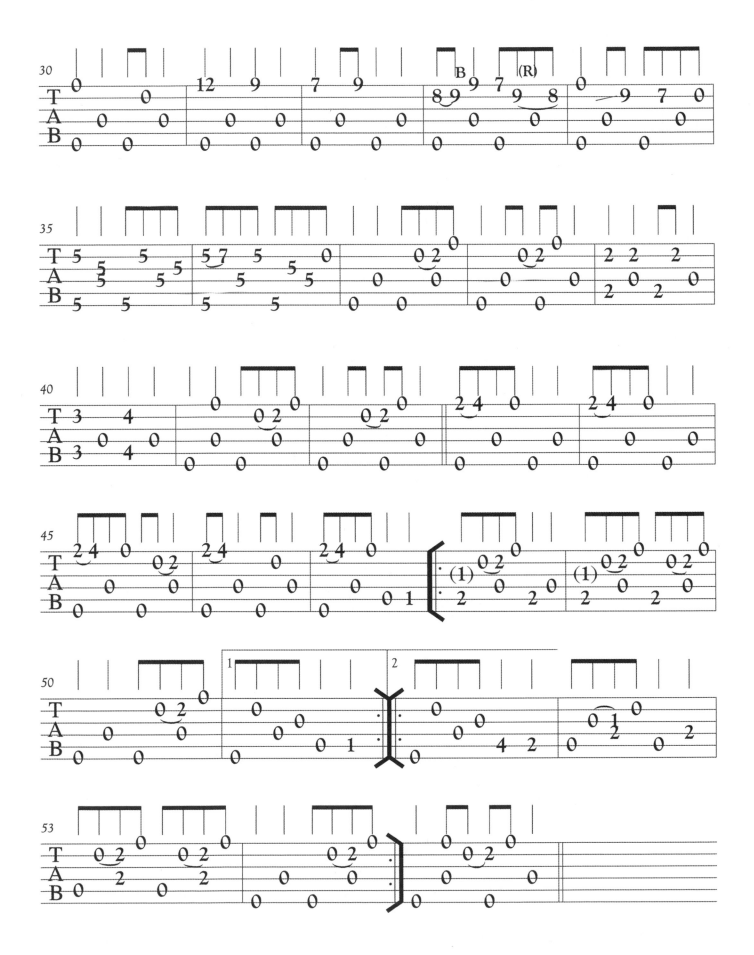

Sailing out of Sebastopol
Part III

Guitar Tuning
D A D F# A D

Trad. arr. Doc Rossi

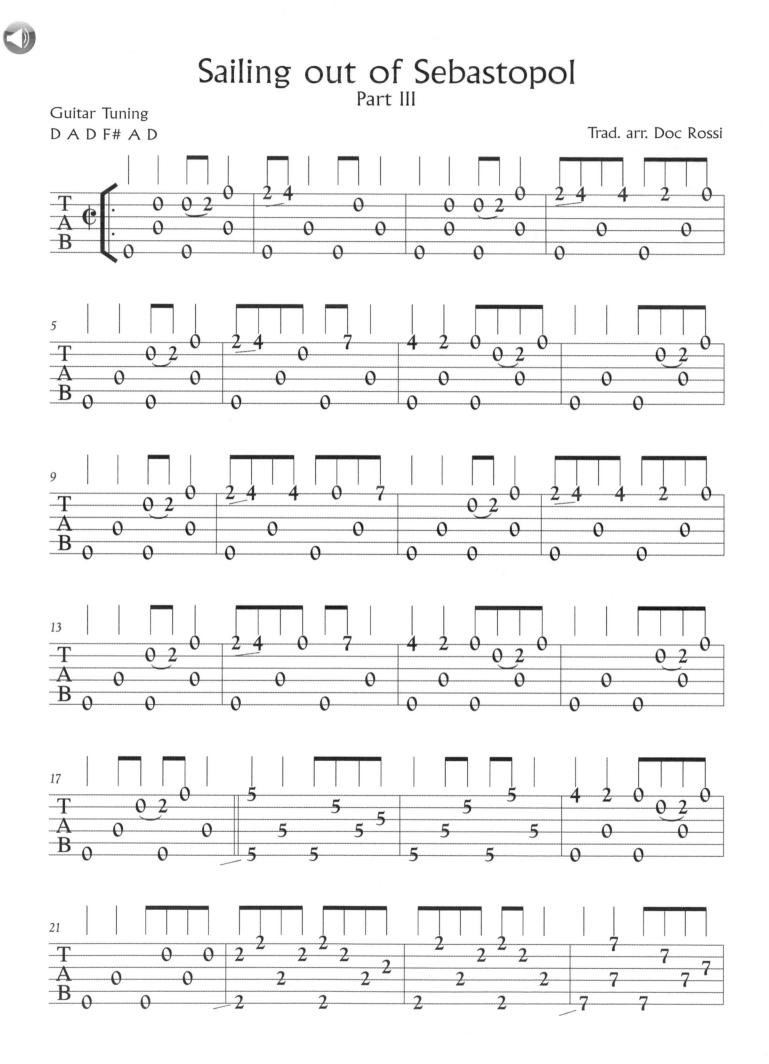

28

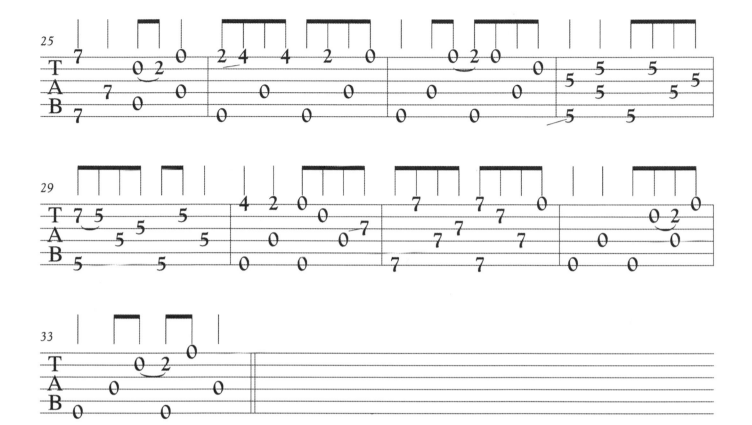

Homage to Clarence White

Guitar Tuning
D A D F# A D

Doc Rossi

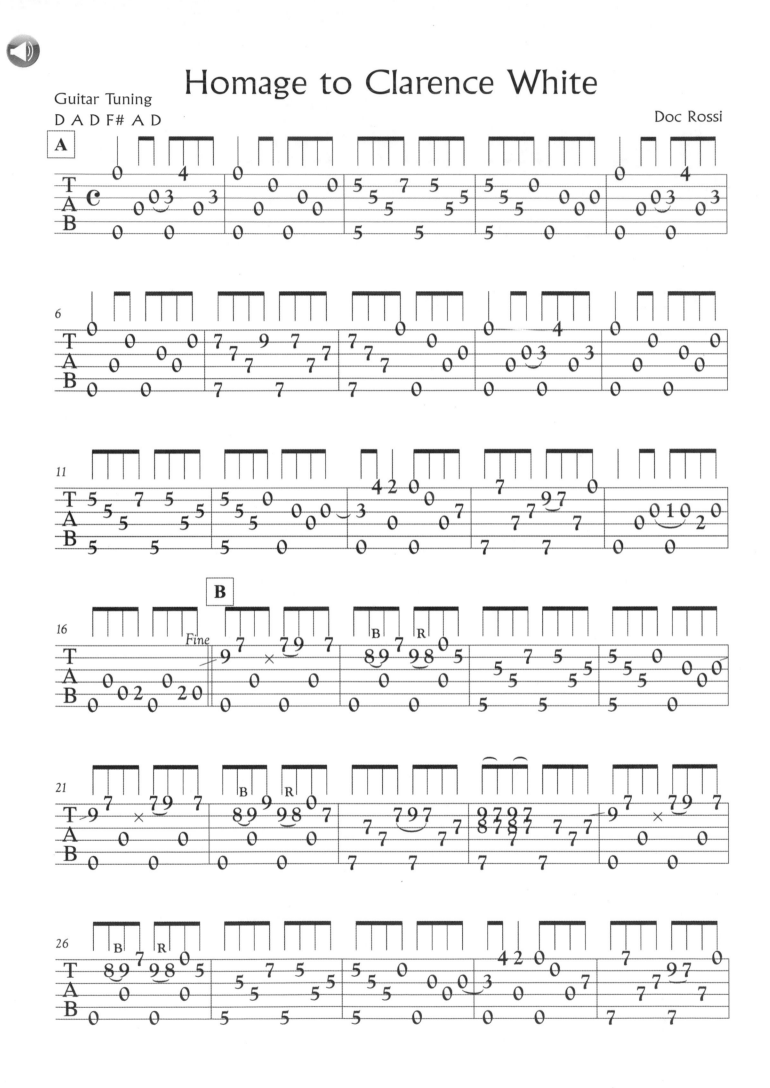

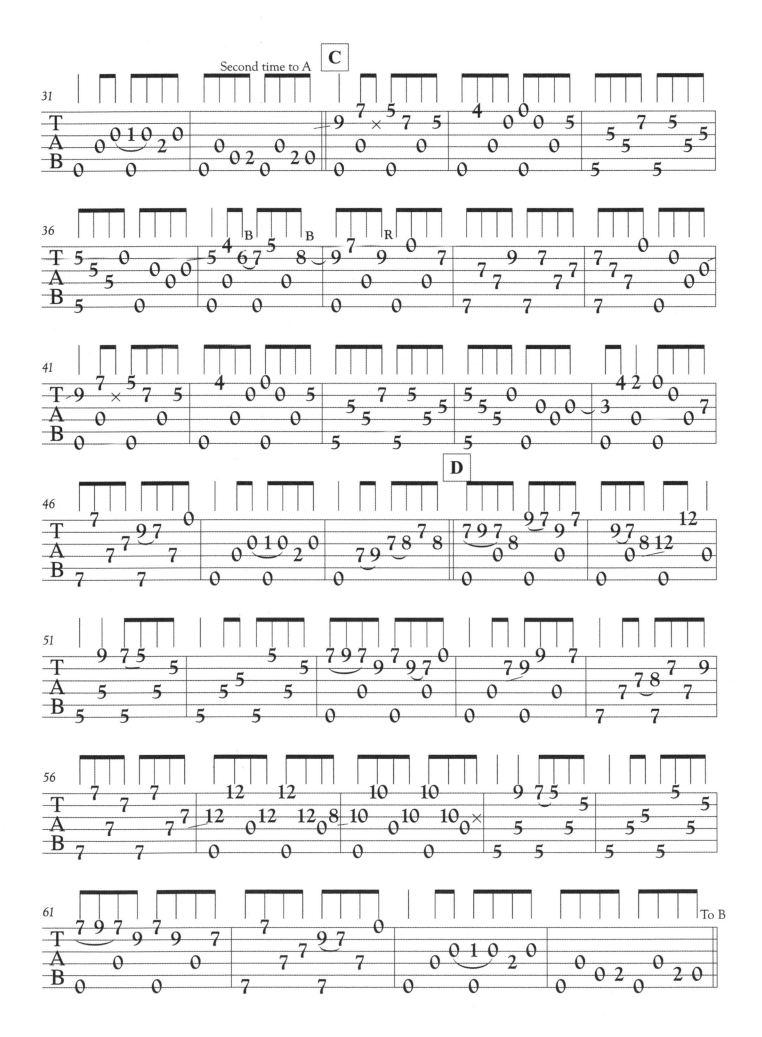

From the Mysterious South

For Norman & Nancy Blake

Guitar Tuning
D A D F# A D

Doc Rossi

Kettle Drum

Guitar Tuning
D A D F# A D

Trad. arr. Doc Rossi

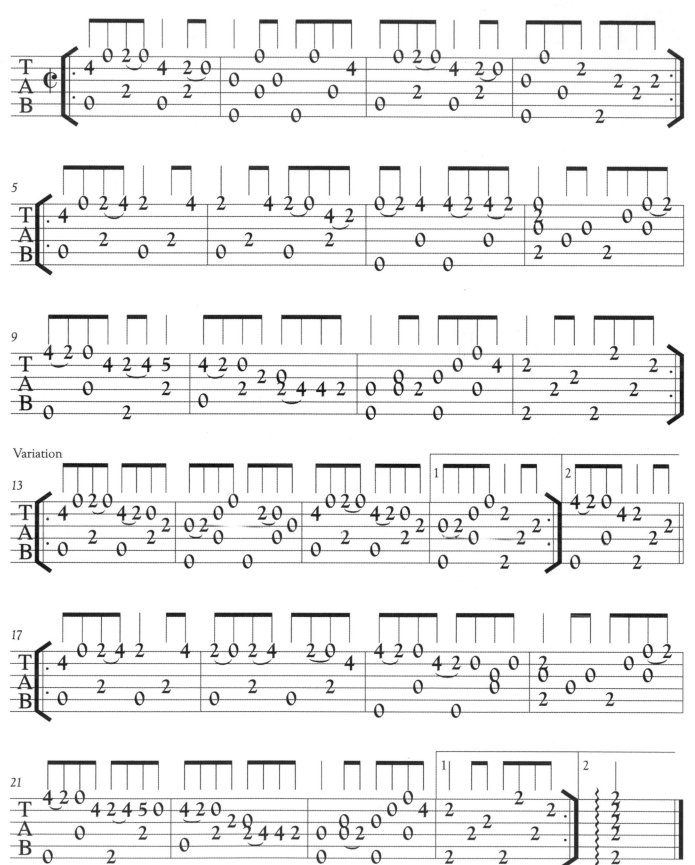

D Modal - D A D G A D

The story Davy Graham told me about DADGAD is that he invented it while visiting Morocco and trying to jam with local musicians. A couple of years later he recorded a stunning version of "She Moves through the Fair" live at The Troubadour that effortlessly blends the traditional Irish melody with eastern improvization. Other guitarists started using DADGAD, and now it is a standard tuning for Celtic-based music. One of the first Irish musicians to use the tuning was Mícheál Ó Domhnaill; one of the first rock musicians was Jimmy Page, who was influenced by Davy and Bert Jansch, who also used the tuning. One of the first finger-style guitarists to use DADGAD extensively was Pierre Bensusan, who eventually made it his standard tuning. Today, almost any guitarist associated with Celtic music uses DADGAD, and even if it is strongly associated with Celtic music, it works very well in almost any genre.

Cailín Deas Cruíte Na mBó

A traditional 18c Irish ballad, sung in Gaelic, that has remained popular. The title in English is "A Pretty Maid Milking her Cow." An updated swing version sung by Judy Garland in the 1940 film *Little Nellie Kelly* may account for the song being so popular on St. Patrick's Day in the USA. My setting is more moody, incorporating a bit of dissonance.

Charade

A slightly dark ballad written in Haute Savoie in the autumn of 2010 while I was pondering how words are one thing, and actions arising from committment are quite another. It's a very straight-forward piece of finger picking.

An original Celtic guitar: 18c cittern by Thomas Perry of Dublin

The Dancing Master of Bosa

This piece is in the key of G. Dedicated to my old friend Angelo Pisanu, the actual Dancing Master of Bosa, this piece uses elements of traditional Sardinian dance music. A characteristic feature of this music is repetition of a melodic phrase three times: first the phrase is played with an open ending, then it is repeated exactly, or almost exactly, with the same open ending, then it is repeated again but with a closed ending. I haven't put in all of the hammer-ons and pull-offs so as to keep the music uncluttered. Use them wherever you like.

These Are My Rivers

Another DADGAD piece in the key of G, "These Are My Rivers" is an attempt to sound like a river flowing gently but persistently to wherever it leads. The title comes from a poem by the Italian poet Giuseppe Ungaretti, which was translated into English by Lawrence Ferlinghetti.

It's partly improvisatory in that there are three main sections, plus a fourth, contrasting section, that are based on picking patterns. These sections can be varied and/or extended as you like.

The Clinton, where I grew up among turtles, muskrats, dragon flies and mosquitoes; The Au Sable and The Tahquamenon of my first travels; The Thames, The Tevere, The Rhone, The Rhine, where I have lived and made music, and The Douro, my new home running into the Atlantic, and where this collection of guitar pieces was put together - these are my rivers.

Cailín Deas Crúite Na mBó

Guitar Tuning
D A D G A D

Trad. arr. Doc Rossi

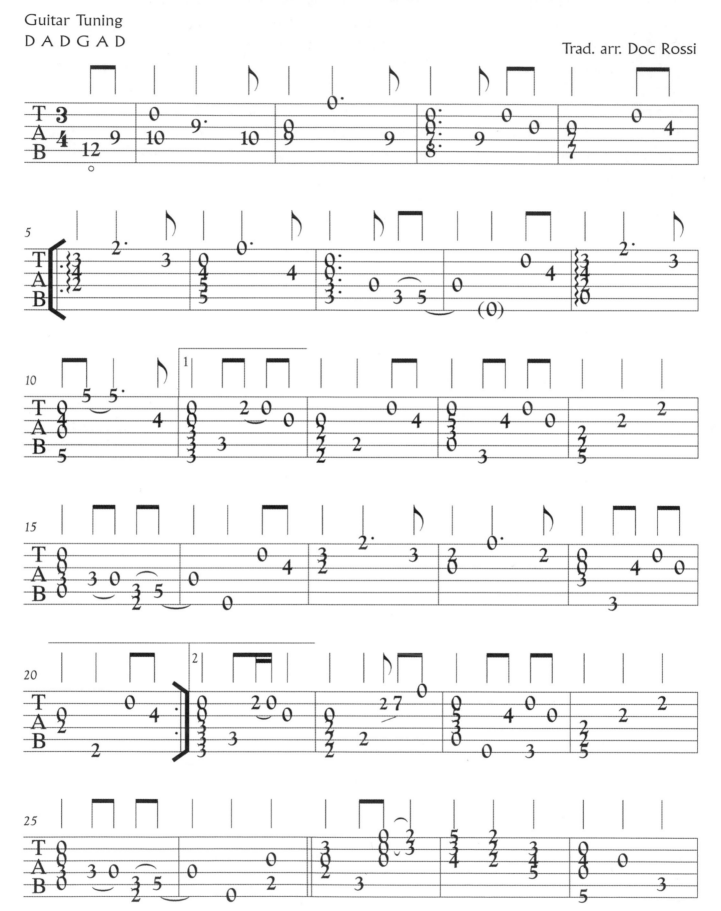

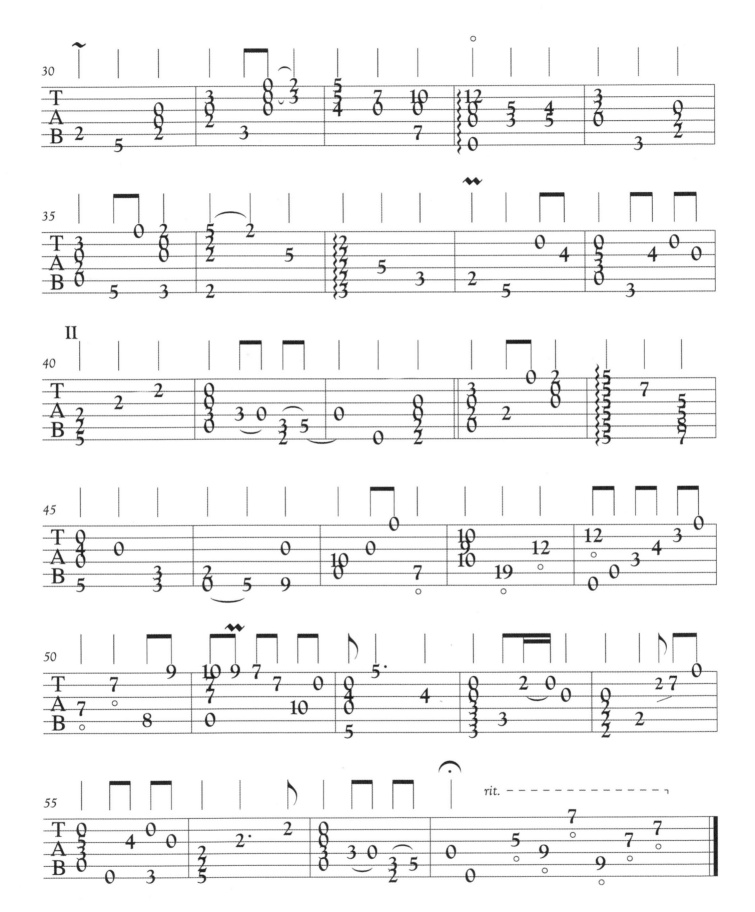

Charade

Guitar Tuning
D A D G A D

Doc Rossi

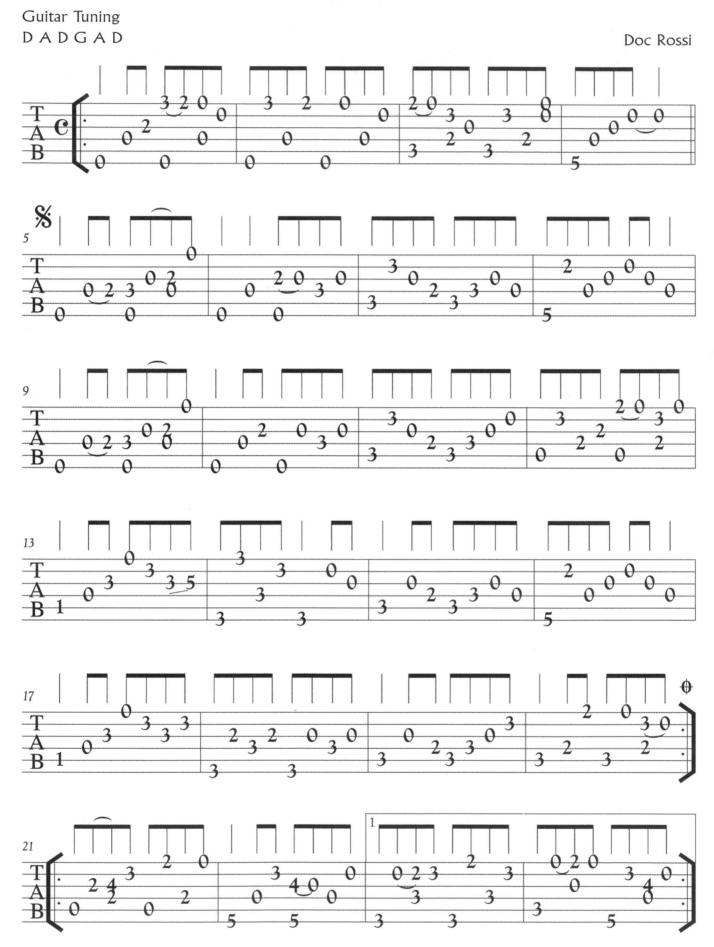

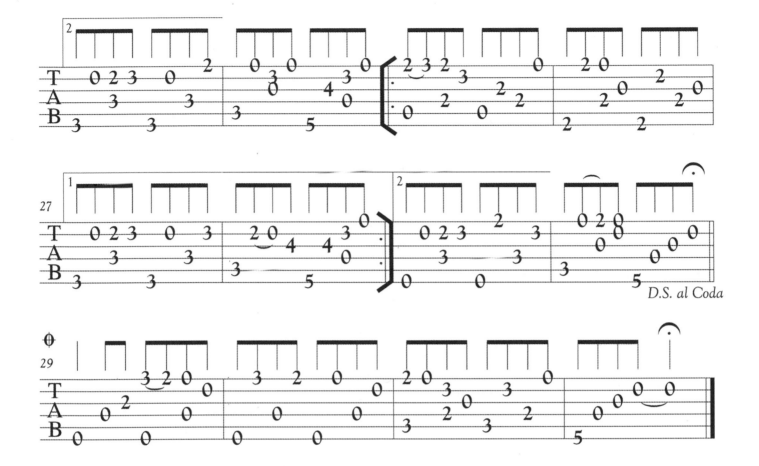

D.S. al Coda

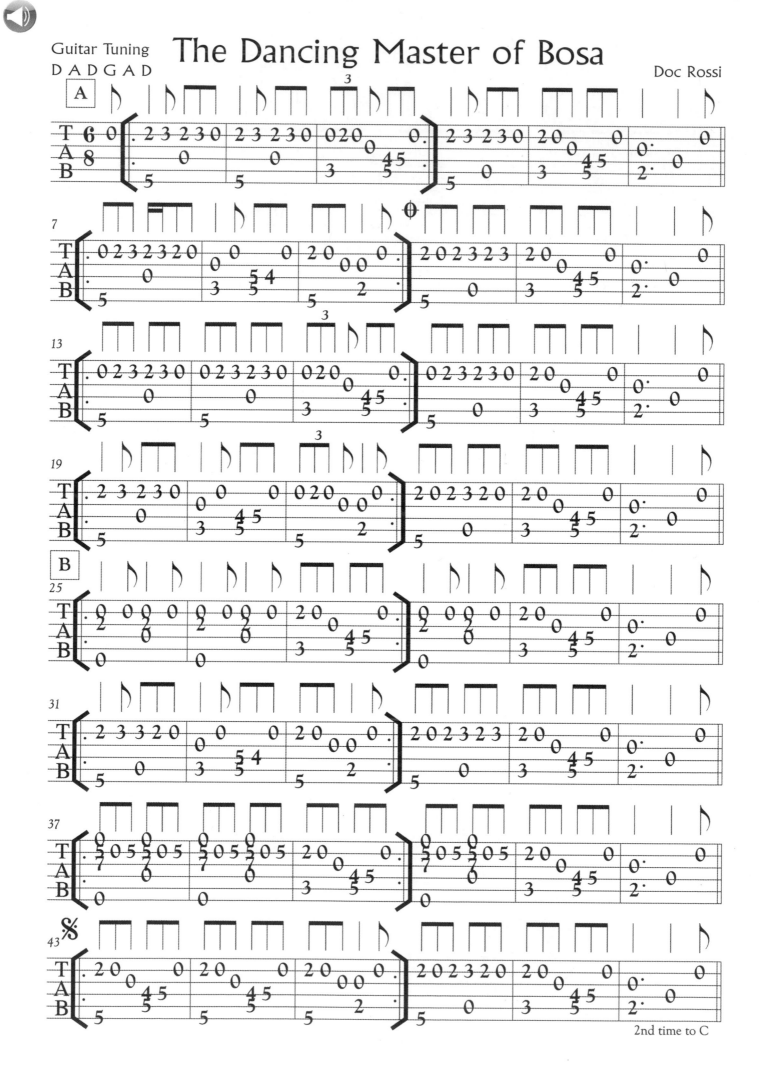

2nd time to C

40

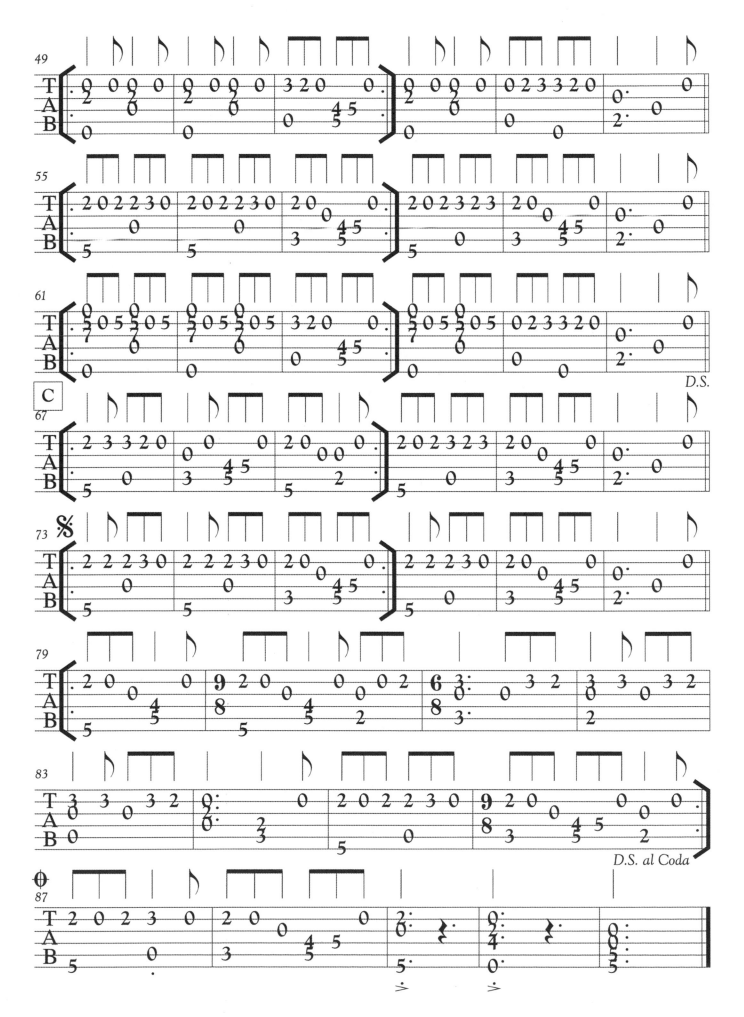

These Are My Rivers

Guitar Tuning
D A D G A D

Doc Rossi

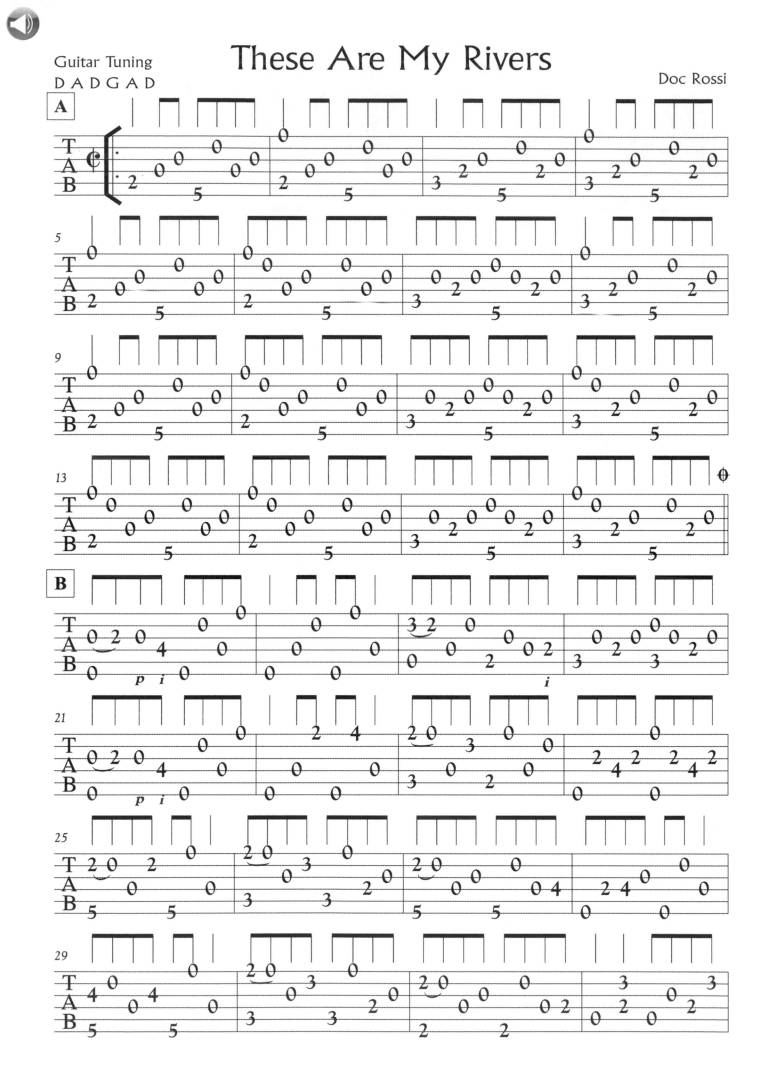

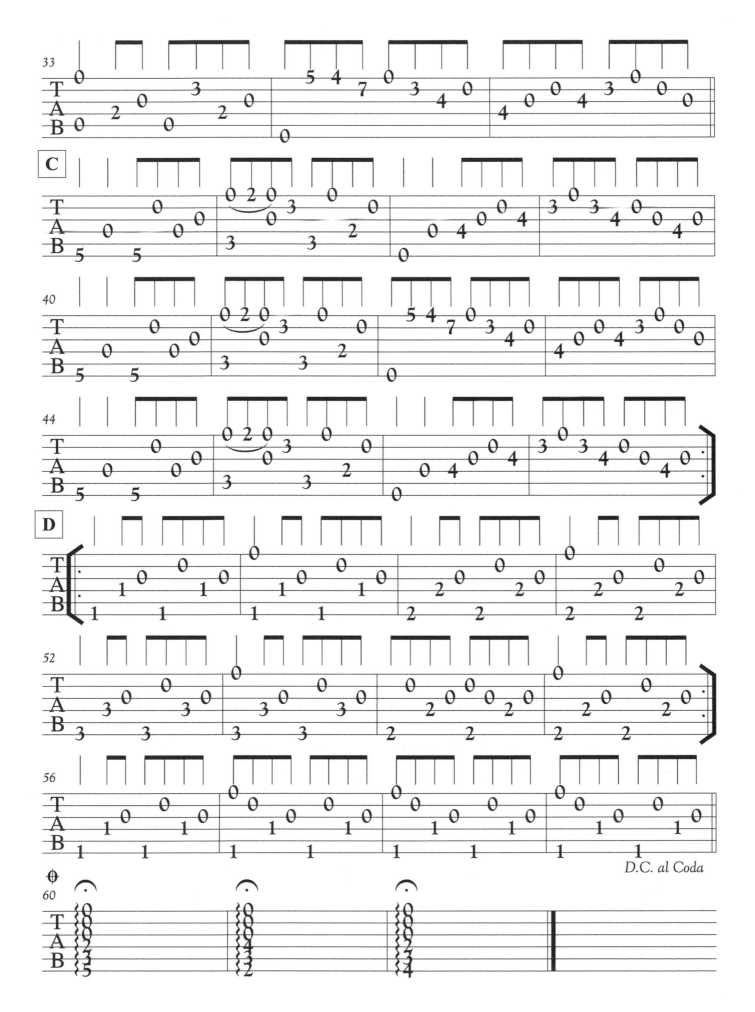

D.C. al Coda

43

D Wahine - D A D F# A C#

Wahine means woman in Hawai'ian, and all *wahine* tunings are in effect a Major 7th chord. Two other common *Wahine* tunings are G - D G D F# B D - and C - C G C G B E. There are several others. *Wahine* tunings give a piece a natural swing as the tune moves from the leading tone to the root note, quite often using a hammer-on at the end of the bar.

Opae Tumatuma

The first Slack Key album I bought was Leonard Kwan's "red album" on Tradewinds, and what a fortunate find that was. Leonard's playing is almost classical in its poise and clarity. "Opae Tumatuma" first appeared on his 1974 Tradewinds LP *The Old Way*.

Leonard was a very precise player who used a wide variety of tunings. On his early albums, he played a Gibson L5, which added to the elegance of his sound.

Opae Tumatuma

Guitar Tuning
D A D F# A C#

Leonard Kwan
arr. Doc Rossi

More Great Books from Doc Rossi...

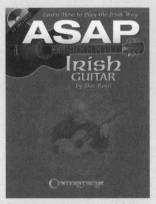
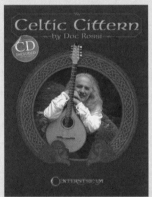
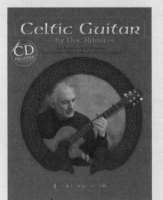